Contents

Dragonflies are **dazzling!**

Marvellous Minibeasts!

DAZZLING
Dragonflies

by Catherine Ipcizade

Consultant:
Laura Jesse
Director, Plant and Insect Diagnostic Clinic
Iowa State University Extension
Ames, Iowa, USA

• • •

raintree
a Capstone company — publishers for children

Raintree is an imprint of Capstone Global Library Limited, a company incorporated in England and Wales having its registered office at 7 Pilgrim Street, London, EC4V 6LB – Registered company number: 6695582

www.raintree.co.uk
myorders@raintree.co.uk

Text © Capstone Global Library Limited 2017
The moral rights of the proprietor have been asserted.

ISBN 978 1 4747 3603 9 (hardback)
20 19 18 17 16
10 9 8 7 6 5 4 3 2 1

ISBN 978 1 4747 3607 7 (paperback)
21 20 19 18 17
10 9 8 7 6 5 4 3 2 1

British Library Cataloguing in Publication Data
A full catalogue record for this book is available from the British Library.

Editorial credits
Editor, Abby Colich; Designer, Bobbie Nuytten; Media Researcher, Jo Miller; Production Specialist, Tori Abraham

Acknowledgements
Alamy: Wong Hock weng, 23; Dreamstime: 57920346, 30 (all); Minden Pictures: John Abbott, 18, NPL/Paul Harcourt Davies, 21; Nature Picture Library: Aflo, 22; Science Source: B.G. Thomson, 28; Shutterstock: Abeselom Zerit, 1, David Byron Keener, 19, Dennis van de Water, 24, Gerald A. DeBoer, 9, Jan-Nor Photography, 5 (bottom left), Jayne Gulbrand, 8, Judith Lienert, 11, 17, kesipun, 4, KPL, 5 (top), kurt_G, 10, Paul Reeves Photography, 14, 15, 27, paulrommer, 5 (bottom right), Peter Eggermann, 6, 7, Puwadol Jaturawutthichai, map (throughout), Richard A McMillin, cover, 13, RODINA OLENA, back cover (background), SDeming, 26, Simon_g, 25, Yongkiet Jitwattanatam, 16, Yuval Heifman, 12, SuperStock: Juniors, 20; UIG via Getty Images: Auscape/Contributor, 29

Printed and bound in India.

Zoom! A dragonfly flutters by. Its two pairs of wings move quickly. Its huge eyes search for food. The dragonfly spots a bug. Gulp! It swallows its prey.

Dragonflies can be bright colours. Some have cool spots or patterns. These insects will dazzle you!

Broad-bodied **chaser**

male

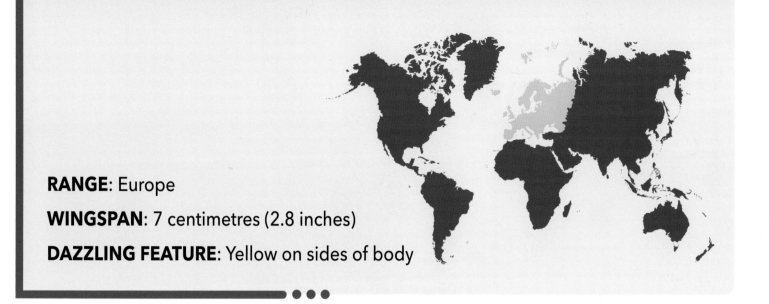

RANGE: Europe

WINGSPAN: 7 centimetres (2.8 inches)

DAZZLING FEATURE: Yellow on sides of body

Chomp! The broad-bodied chaser eats a bug. Then it flies back to its perch. This dragonfly likes to hang out in one spot. It waits there for the next bug.

This dragonfly's body is thick and flat. A male's body is light blue. A female's body is yellow or brown. Both have bright yellow on their sides.

female

Calico pennant

male

RANGE: United States and Canada

WINGSPAN: 6 cm (2.4 in.)

DAZZLING FEATURE: Heart-shaped spots

What shapes are on the calico pennant's back? Hearts! Red hearts run down a male's back. A female has yellow hearts running down her back. These dragonflies have black bodies. Colourful spots mark their wings.

female

Crimson marsh glider

RANGE: Asia

LENGTH: 3 cm (1.2 in.)

DAZZLING COLOUR: Bright pink

Wow! The male crimson marsh glider stands out. His body is bright pink! His face is red. A female is gold or brown. Look at their wings. They are transparent. Coloured veins run through them.

veins

Flame skimmer

RANGE: Parts of the United States and Mexico

WINGSPAN: 4.5 cm (1.8 in.)

DAZZLING COLOUR: Bright orange

Can you guess what colour the flame skimmer is? Males are bright orange, just like flames. Females are brown. Their wings are transparent with brown edges.

Flame skimmers like it hot. They live where it's warm. Some even live near hot springs.

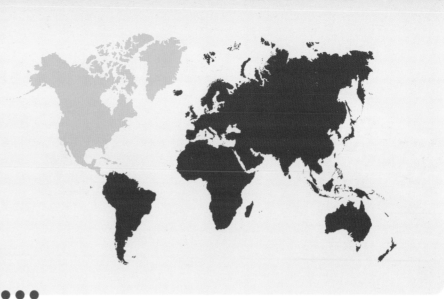

RANGE: North America

WINGSPAN: 8 cm (3.2 in.)

DAZZLING FEATURE: Target
  mark on head

Zoom! Green darners are fast. They fly up to 56 kilometres (35 miles) per hour. At the end of summer, they fly south. Huge swarms travel together. Then they mate. Some of the offspring fly north in spring.

See the mark on the top of its head? The mark looks like a target.

Fulvous forest skimmer

female

Those are some bold wings! The fulvous forest skimmer's wings are mostly coloured. Only the tips are transparent. Males are red with brown heads. Females are rust coloured. This dragonfly lives in forests. It sticks to areas that are moist. Skimmers do a lot of hunting. They fly around looking for food.

RANGE: India

WINGSPAN: 6 cm (2.4 in.)

DAZZLING FEATURE: Coloured wings

male

Halloween pennant

RANGE: United States and Canada

WINGSPAN: 6 cm (2.4 in.)

DAZZLING COLOURS: Yellow-orange and black or brown

Boo! The Halloween pennant is yellow-orange and black or brown. It perches on top of bushes or tall grass. Whoosh! Wind blows the plant. The dragonfly moves with it. The insect looks like a pennant, or flag, as it sways. This dragonfly is strong. It can fly in heavy wind and rain.

RANGE: Europe

WINGSPAN: 6 cm (2.4 in.)

DAZZLING COLOURS: Red and
  yellow

· · ·

What's this dragonfly's mouth full of?
Bugs! The ruddy darter can hold eight
fruit flies in its mouth at once. Ruddy
darters like water with lots of plants.
Larvae spend a year under water.
Adults are yellow. Males turn red as
they age.

Scarlet dwarf

male

RANGE: Asia

WINGSPAN: 2 cm (0.8 in.)

DAZZLING SKILL: Handstands

What's that dragonfly doing? A handstand! It's a hot day. The scarlet dwarf lifts its tail end towards the sky. The rest of its body stays cool.

This dragonfly is the world's smallest. It's about the size of your fingertip. The male's tiny body is red. A female is white, yellow and brown.

female

Phantom flutterer

RANGE: Africa, Middle East

LENGTH: 3.6 cm (1.4 in.)

DAZZLING FEATURE: Bright colours on wings

Ooh! Can you see those bright colours? A phantom flutterer sports purple, blue or red on its wings. Its body is blue. The bright colours shine in the light. Flutterers get their name because they fly like butterflies.

Twelve-spotted skimmer

female

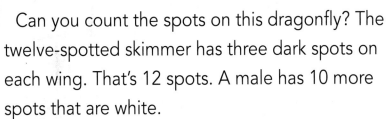

RANGE: United States and Canada

WINGSPAN: 10.2 cm (4 in.)

DAZZLING FEATURE: Spots on wings

Can you count the spots on this dragonfly? The twelve-spotted skimmer has three dark spots on each wing. That's 12 spots. A male has 10 more spots that are white.

A male watches over his territory. Another male comes near. They fly in loops around each other. One male flies away, confused. The other male wins the territory.

male

Wandering percher

What's that flash of red? It's a male wandering percher. A female wandering percher dips her tail end into the water. She is laying eggs. The male holds onto her. This keeps other males away.

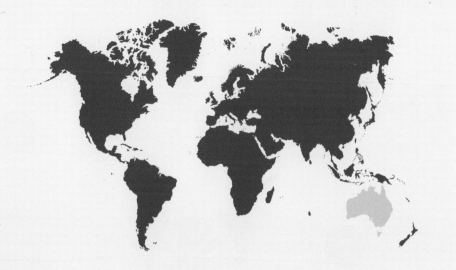

RANGE: Australia

WINGSPAN: 5.6 cm (2.2 in.)

DAZZLING COLOUR: Red

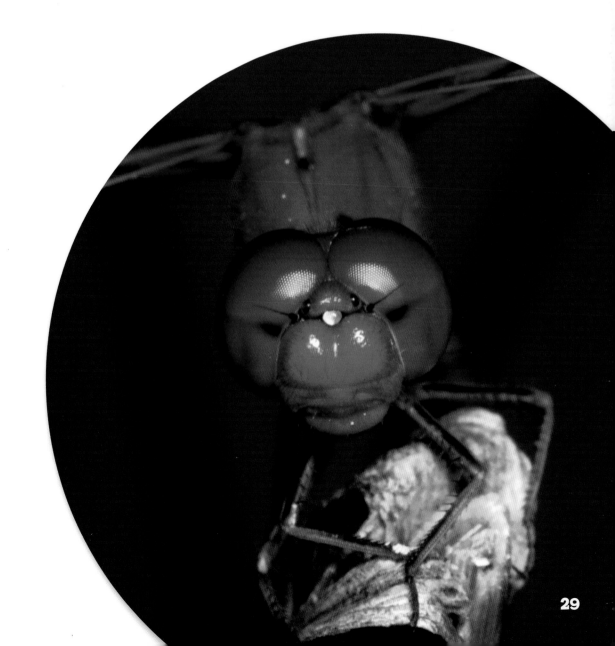

Life cycle of a dragonfly

1

Dragonflies begin life as eggs.

2

A larva, or nymph, hatches from an egg.

3

A nymph moults as it grows into an adult.

4

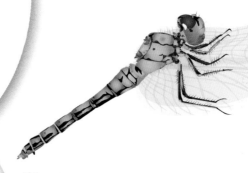

adult dragonfly

Glossary

feature important part or quality of something

flutter wave or flap quickly

hot spring place where warm water comes out of the ground

larva insect at a stage of development between egg and adult

mate join together to produce young

moult shed the hard outer covering while growing

offspring the young of a person, animal or plant

perch high place where a bird or insect can rest and view its surroundings

prey animal hunted by another animal for food

range area where an animal mostly lives

swarm gather or fly close together in a large group

territory area of land that an animal claims as its own to live in

transparent easily seen through

vein small, stiff tube that helps give shape to a bug's wings

Read more

British Insects and Other Minibeasts (Nature in Your Neighbourhood), Clare Collinson (Franklin Watts, 2015)

Incredible Insects (Zoom In On), Richard Spilsbury (Wayland, 2015)

Websites

BBC Nature Dragonflies
www.bbc.co.uk/nature/life/Dragonfly

British Dragonfly Society
www.british-dragonflies.org.uk

Encyclopaedia Britannica
kids.britannica.com/elementary/article-390734/dragonfly?

Comprehension questions

1. How many pairs of wings does a dragonfly have?

2. Page 13 says some flame skimmers live near hot springs. Use the glossary on page 31 to define hot spring.

3. Choose two dragonflies that are discussed in the book. How are they alike? How are they different?

Index